FEARLESS
PUBLIC SPEAKING
A Practical Guide

FEARLESS PUBLIC SPEAKING
A Practical Guide

Cliff
Kepaletswe

ISBN 978-99912-941-2-4
Published by
Cliff Kepaletswe, Botswana
Tel: + 267 71625801
E-mail: cliff.magicwords@gmail.com

Editor: Thebe Makhwa

Designed by Kaytwo Productions
(+267) 3953027

Printed by Printing & Publishing Company Botswana
Plot 5647, Nakedi Road, Broadhurst Ind.
Gaborone Tel:(+267) 3914788

All texts are an original creation by the Author as per his experience and observations.

Contents

Dedication ....

Prologue ....

Preamble ....

Introduction ....

1. Confidence Boosters 17

2. On the Roll 22

3. Reading from a Source 32

4. The Platforms 34

5. Public Address System & Electronic

   Media..37

6. Directing Ceremonies 41

7. The Closure 45

About the Author 47

Author's Note 49

Dedication

This winning package of constructive secrets is wholly dedicated to my strikingly beautiful daughter.

Harepa, although you came at the peak of my tempests, I have faith that very soon God will groom you into a fine young woman who will simply go out of her way to seek and find the blemish-free truth about her past.

Love always

Daddy.

Prologue

Dear Reader,

I am most pleased to usher you into a fresh and technique-studded portal of knowledge on public speaking.

What you are about to experience is a revealing exploration of techniques built from observations and lessons learnt from over fifteen years of active public speaking. My experience was garnered since my days as a university scholar until my time as a television and radio presenter.

I trust you will find this package uplifting enough to catapult you to your long cherished spot in the sun.

Yours

Cliff

Preamble

Of course public speaking is serious business. Like any other well coordinated activity, it requires thorough planning on your part. Firstly, it starts off as an abstract imagination of the forthcoming event in your curious mind. It is very vital and natural that you visualise and imagine the event sometime before the set date. You should relax and play with the mental visuals in however way you wish. This will help psych you up for your big day. Some people may hastily mistake this mental process for a sign of the undesirable feelings of anxiety, but it is not necessarily so. It is just your mind readying itself for the nearing action. This is the stage at which you should be at liberty to play around with possible ideas that may help spice up your forthcoming presentation.

Introduction

For each and every one of us, there is an unavoidable time in our colourful lives when we are expected to make some form of public presentation before a relatively sizeable audience. It may be the heart-wrenching reading of an obituary at a loved one's funeral, making a convincing presentation of a winning business proposal before a team of shrewd prospective clients or even adducing a traumatic piece of incriminating evidence before a full and intimidating court of law. All these diverse scenarios dully constitute the art of public speaking to some extent.

However, for some unknown reason, many people simply dread speaking in public. Maybe the sheer thought of them being the centre of attraction triggers their unsuspecting minds to unleash unbearable feelings of self doubt, insecurity, nervousness or even a panic attack in some extreme cases. Are you one of these people? If you have answered in the affirmative, do not be overly concerned. It is purely natural to succumb to any of these aforementioned feelings. The truth of the matter is this: even the most seasoned public speakers of the world sometimes experience anxiety prior to their definitive moments. All that matters is how you manage to arrest any unsettling feelings of uneasiness, right before you utter the first line of your speech.

It is fairly normal that every human being will need a pillar of strength to see them through the glaring eyes of their eager audience. This abstract source of strength usually varies from one individual to another. Some speakers may draw their strength from a short prayer, a brief session of meditation or even a crackle of their knuckles. One point remains constant: avoid taking any depressants such as alcohol and other habit forming drugs prior to your public speaking session. Drugs will simply make your speech slurry or incoherent, and ultimately leave you with an unwanted short-lived sense of false confidence.

But really, why not just enjoy the thrill of

your fame with a sober mind? After all, public speaking is meant to be enjoyable for both you and your audience.

Remember well, that public speaking is a coordinated and equally sensitive process. Therefore, you need to approach it in a meticulous fashion.

Just like all the other vocal arts such as singing and poetry, speaking also has a formal feel of rhythm that comes into play once your vocal cords start to vibrate and giving you that sense of speech.

Confidence Boosters

Admittedly, one may feel slightly shaken just a few moments from their actual public address. This, after all, is one of the tenets of our humanity. But you will further agree that, in most cases your level of confidence is largely influenced by how you perceive yourself as an individual. Is not it strange, how any deeply embedded negative thoughts of inadequacy may eventually hamper your performance?

Fortunately, you will be pleased to know that you have been armed with the innate ability to elevate your own level of confidence through different methods available at your disposal. These life-saving techniques may be taken advantage of in the following fashion:

Grooming

It is a given that once you are well groomed, you will feel content with yourself because you know that you are of a pleasant demeanour. This comes as a natural feeling of assurance that has a magical effect on your morale and self esteem. You should always strike a well groomed facial appearance for any public speaking engagement. Wear simple or plain hair styles, and avoid cluttering your facial area with too much jewellery as this may distract your audience and divert their attention from the actual presentation.

While it may sound a bit hackeyened, the age-old adage that says, *"you are what you wear"* is loaded in content. Indeed you are. Always dress appropriately for your occasion. Avoid clothes that might make a dramatic or loud fashion statement. All in all, just simply go with the theme of the occasion, and remain pleasant and comfortable. Do not over or under-dress as it may make you feel out of place.

Subject matter knowledge

Feed yourself with as much relevant information as you can on whatever the subject of your address is. This will naturally elevate your sense of confidence. If it requires that you carry out some intensive research to acquire information, please do so adequately because it will pay dividends once you are under the spotlight. An informed speaker never runs out of sensible and relevant material to share. In some cases, you may realise that your audience know less than you do on the subject at hand. On this note, this knowledge should inherently help you settle down and appreciate that you are at the helm of the event. This is usually common in media conferences.

The feel good attitude

Feelings play a very key role in the successful performance of any function that requires one's application of diligence. It is paramount that you foster a "*feel good about yourself attitude*," moments before your actual address. Most of all, remind yourself about any of your notable past achievements. This will help arouse feelings of self-worth, and in the end translate into high levels of morale, self esteem and confidence.

Practice

Practice is one noble universal principle that is flexibly applicable to the growth of any practitioner to a level of mastery in their respective craft. Hence, the maxim that says, "*practice makes perfect.*" If you want to grow into a well rounded and confident public speaker, you need to, first of all, nurture the passion by wilfully taking advantage of any available opportunity to speak at any given gathering. Regular practice is exactly what you need to help you garner more experience and skills, which will in turn help you discover your true style of speaking.

**CHAPTER
TWO**

On the Roll

Finally, your dreaded and deciding moment is here. You have been preparing yourself in several strategic ways to help enhance your confidence. This is certainly your moment to shine bright. Indeed you will shine, and make yourself and everyone proud if you carefully engage the right public speaking techniques.

Breaking the ice

When you are on stage, you may probably feel that invisible but uncomfortable dividing line between you and your audience. This barrier is called "ice." It is your natural duty as a speaker to break it and gain access into the seemingly hostile world of your audience. Breaking the ice does not require any magical formula. No matter how tense and serious an audience may seem, you do not always need rib cracking humour to get through to them. You may choose to avoid jokes at all costs, especially if you are unsure about their suitability. A bad joke may out-rightly mar your soon-to-be moment of glory. Be your natural self. If you have come prepared with a very powerful and captivating piece of introduction, then you may have a field day. Catchy introductions usually stay memorable in the minds of your listeners, which may win you their loyalty until the end of your speech. Please, do not make the mistake of forgetting to send a line of greetings to the audience, but it should come at a strategic point in your ice breaking process. Send a sincere smile and the audience will realise that indeed you are a part of them. Remember, a smile is reported to have the ability to start many. It is infectious!

Originality

You probably have a person or people that you hold in high esteem with regards to their exceptional public speaking skills. However, do not let your admiration of those great speakers dilute your own uniqueness. Be yourself, and do not be tempted to copy another speaker's style because each individual has been gifted with their peculiar manner of address. By emulating, you are simply committing the crime of denying the world the rare opportunity of unearthing that great and fearless speaker in you. Maintain your originality, you might surprise yourself and discover that you are a new and deeply unique breed of a public speaker in the arena.

Choice of language of address

If in any way you happen to have the liberty to choose the language of proceedings, please ensure that you settle for a language that you and the audience are most comfortable with.

Language purity and consistency

Once you have started addressing your audience using a particular language, keep it that way until the end of your session. Display proficiency through consistency in language use. Take advantage of this rare moment and earn accolades by showcasing your linguistic prowess. Switching from one language code to the other within one presentation simply makes you appear unprofessional and indecisive. Even if you lack the right word to express or emphasise on a particular point, avoid borrowing from another language because it comes off as untidy. You may rather pause and let the word come naturally. Try more to relax, it will help your mind operate with ease.

Punchy and persuasive words

As a public speaker, you need to make a permanent imprint in the hearts of your audience. However, you need to work hard and earn this. You may have noticed that there are some people who possess the rare but effortless ability of sending the whole audience into a roar of applause each time they speak. There is not much to this though, the secret lies discreetly with their choice of words as they speak. In the world of words, there are some words which are technically more emphatic and persuasive than others. Such a use of words is usually common within the peculiar industries of marketing and advertising. Now, if you want to match up, get yourself in the habit of growing your vocabulary, and learn the punchy and persuasive synonyms of the everyday words that you use and you will see a remarkable change in the way your audience receives you each time you speak. Take for instance, a word like *beautiful*. It is less persuasive than its synonyms: magnificent, fantastic and spectacular.

Avoid anchors

To further polish and add a smooth professional touch to your speaking, you need to move away from the constant usage of certain sounds, words and phrases as anchors in between your sentences whilst you are still pondering about the next line of words to deliver. Non-linguistic anchors are a difficult habit to drop once developed. These are some of the common and irritating anchors that a lot of people are struggling to shed off their speech: *"ehhh," "mhhh," "you know" and "you know what I'm saying."* Anchors are undesirable, and they do a great job at spoiling the smooth flow and appearance of your speech. Do note, however, It is permissible to pause for a while in the event you suddenly grow blank in search of the right words to use. However, ensure not to make your pauses inordinately long

Body language

There is no shade of doubt, that body language in the form of gestures and other bodily movements make up a part of any human language. You certainly cannot restrict your body from making movements when you speak; you would seem very unnatural and stiff. After all, some of the movements come as a reflex. When engaged in public speaking, keep the body movements minimal, neatly coordinated and synchronized with your verbal expressions. A word of caution: do not let your body language get in the way of your speech. At times, overly engaged bodily movements are construed as a sign of nervousness.

The use of body language would usually be most appropriate when you need to emphasise a point. For instance, you may demonstrate the movement or the shape of something with the use of your hands. This is fairly permissible and goes to show that you are relaxed.

At all times, be mindful of your posture whenever you speak. Always maintain an upright position with your head up high. Be firm and do not slouch.

Eye contact

Pivotal to your success and growth as a public speaker, is how much eye contact you establish with your audience each time you face them. Although there will be several pairs of eyes all glued on yours, do not in any way fret. The eyes is where your natural charm lies. Ensure to make the deliberate effort of arresting your audience with your God given charisma.   Human beings are much aware of the sure fact that your confidence is judged from your ability to maintain eye contact. Do not feel intimidated by the many eyes in the room, but make it your task to rather captivate them with your piercing eye contact. Gently rove your eyes from one end of the room to the other, but taking care not to appear arrogant. Looking into the eyes of your audience automatically creates an endearing connection between you and them.

Audibility and voice projection

Being audible can be quite a challenge if you find yourself having to address a large audience in a very roomy venue or in the outdoors without the aid of a public address system. Ensure to project your voice to a pleasant pitch and maintain a particular octave. To further enhance your audibility, you need to articulate all your words clearly at a steady pace.

Rhythm

Establish and maintain a rhythm of speech that will permit you to articulate your words clearly, coherently and audibly. Do not get carried away by the rapid flow of words as your presentation intensifies and speed up the tempo of your rhythm. To avoid being carried away in the midst of your flow of speech, you can improvise a gentle and subtle mechanism to guide you into a constant pace by complementing your verbal activity. For instance, one may use a slight tap of the foot. But this should be done with all care taken not to disrupt you and the audience. Do not get lost in your own world of perceived excellence and jumble up your words.

Time management

It is very vital for you as a speaker to adhere strictly to your allocated time of presentation. Learn to summarise and prune your content into salient points to allow you a well timed speech. People who prepare their presentations in the form of well summarised pointers usually enjoy their time speaking in public, because this technique allows them to relax and speak in a slightly informal and comfortable mode.

Reading from a source

The public presentation of information from another source or medium can be a challenge to any speaker. You need to appreciate that a full exercise of the several techniques suggested in the previous chapters may not be adequately applicable. For example, you will find yourself struggling to maintain eye contact and read at the same time. The best way to go about it is to familiarize yourself with the full information prior to the presentation. Once you have internalised the information from the source, then you do not need to read it word by word on the day of your presentation. You may take a bold chance and read only the   first few phrases and follow them up with a raise of your eyes to scan the audience whilst you complete the sentences with paraphrases of the context. But most importantly, be cautious not to temper with factual details such as figures, dates, demographics and so forth.

Do not sound stiff like a typical reader , relax and give your presentation an active voice. You can only acquire that smooth flow if you had afforded yourself ample time to have a thorough study of the information. But you do not necessarily need to memorize the contents. Be as natural as you can be in your address.

Avoid looking down on your source of information for a prolonged period of time.

**CHAPTER
FOUR**

The Platforms

Public speaking is a form of performance. The speaker, being the centre of attention needs to be in a place where he or she will be fully visible to the audience. There are several platforms that are used to provide the public speaker with that point of operation.

Podium

As one of the many platforms used in public speaking, the podium happens to be a favourite for many. It is very necessary that a larger part of your upper body remains visible whenever you are making any

34

addresses from behind a podium. Evidently, the podium provides a physical support structure that you may take advantage of in improving your stance as you address your public. The podium offers you a flat firm surface that you could use to rest your hands on as you speak. But do not be overly dependent for support on the podium. You should feel free to engage in the natural body language such as gestures where appropriate. You may as well make some controlled movements away from the podium, but ensure not to stay too far away from it for too long, lest it loses its meaning. Some podiums may be a bit taller in build, request for a platform to elevate yourself if you are a person of short build.

Open stage

As opposed to the podium, speaking from an open stage or platform can turn out to be rough if you are a novice public speaker. This position exposes your entire body to the audience. In this instance, you have absolutely no physical structure to lean on or hide behind for support, but only your confidence.

For a good impression and great control of your session, maintain a central position on the platform. Do not make unnecessary regular movements. But slight and well calculated movements from left to right may work. Too much movement on the platform may also expose you to the looming danger of tripping and falling, hence the need to keep it minimal.

CHAPTER
FIVE

Public Address System & Electronic Media

Many public speakers become unsure about the quality of their voices once they hear themselves through the speakers of a public address system, especially if it is their first time to use one. It is important that you visit the venue well in time and liaise with the system operators or technicians to help you acclimatise yourself with the whole set of equipment. Carry out a sound check for your voice if it is possible.

A public address system is technically equipped with an amplifier, which serves to provide an even broadcast of your voice throughout the whole venue. On this note, it is not necessary for you to exert pressure on your voice. Do not pitch your voice beyond its natural octave as it will spoil the beauty of your speech by causing it to unpleasantly rumble through the sound speakers. Speak at your natural level of voice, and make public speaking effortless and fun. Allow the technical team to guide you on the appropriate distance to maintain from the microphone during your speech. At times, if you speak too close to the microphone the system speakers may produce an irritating "pop" sound as you articulate words that begin with plosives. Also, if you are too far, the microphone may not pick the waves from your voice adequately. Microphones have a voice activated device and once you have identified that appropriate distance to maintain, it will produce a pleasant and crystal clear sound through the speakers.

Visual aids

The availability of aids such as PowerPoint and other visuals can conveniently relieve you of the heavy burden of being the main point of focus. But the aids do not avert your responsibilities of controlling the presentation. You are still expected to do most of the talking. Let your speaking be in sync with your visual display. And it may also help to have an assistant who will help operate the information source as you do the speaking. Maintain a neutral position that will not get in the way of the projection of the images on the screen. The use of an infrared pointer may also help you have it easy navigating around the projected images of your presentation.

On radio

When on radio, it is unnecessary for you to pitch your voice beyond its natural octave, lest you will be labelled as trying too hard to impress the listeners. One other thing, the sound of your own voice on the studio headphones may also tempt you to take an unwise cosmetic stance of trying to shape and polish your voice to suit the perceived radio standards. You will only sound absurd and irritating, but rather engage your everyday voice and energy.

On television

Television is the high end of all electronic media. We cannot emphasise enough, the need for you to look your best in your overall grooming for any televised public address. Fortunately, the Television crew is usually helpful in advising you on the ideal appearance for the particular broadcast you may be identified for. You may like to liaise with them regarding your ideal appearance. However, remain calm at all times during the television broadcast, and most of all, do not seem too obviously conscious of the cameras around you. Some speakers exaggerate their body language and talk incessantly as a deliberate effort to impress the viewers. This is very unattractive as opposed to your natural demeanour of speech.

Directing Ceremonies

Once you have elevated your level of confidence to celestial heights, you will find it much easier and more enjoyable to spend most of your time addressing crowds of people as their Director of Ceremonies.

Directing of ceremonies is not simply about sending your audience into fits of laughter with your rib cracking jokes. Yes, humour may be applicable, but make a thorough assessment of the occasion. Moreover, study the laid down programme well and adhere to it. There is undoubtedly more to this part of public speaking.

As a Director of Ceremonies, you need to be well researched and equally knowledgeable on the theme of the Ceremony. Be reasonably conversant with the jargon of the particular gathering. For example, if it is doctors, you may learn some of their commonly used terminology, and apply it where relevant in your speech. This will help show that you are a well rounded and versatile speaker.

If possible, have an insight of the credentials, professions et cetera of the people that constitute the audience, to help you attune a style of address suitable to their standards.

You should do more than just ushering of speakers and activities. Provide a professional sense of bridge to help blend speakers and activities that follow one another. This works well in killing the monotony of calling speaker after speaker or one activity after the other.

It is the duty of the Director of Ceremonies to school the audience on basic housekeeping protocols. Therefore, it is crucial hospitality that the audience be advised on items such as directions to restrooms, restaurant, tea time et cetera.

The Closure

Whatever the purpose of the gathering may have been, the fact is, you have a standing obligation as the speaker to show gratitude to your gathering for their invaluable audience. Find the basic words to express how thankful you are for their attention, you would have fulfilled your moral conviction. You can even go the extra mile and take a bow before the crowd as you walk off the stage.

About the Author

Cliff Kepaletswe is a very discerning and seasoned public speaker, television and radio host with a knack for captivating public presentations. He is a proven language purist with the rare ability to reach and maintain a native speaker's level of eloquence in both English and Setswana.

Amongst many of his public speaking achievements, he is notably credited for launching, as a presenter, Botswana Television's first family talk show, *Molemo wa Kgang* in 2006. Owing to his extraordinary oratory skills, Cliff turned the show into a household name within a period of six months after its launch.

He is currently involved with a local radio station, Duma FM, as a talk & music show presenter where he is fast gaining favour with listeners. Over and above his involvement with the electronic media, Cliff has also proved his mettle as a prolific public speaker in an endless list of high profile

events that he has excellently facilitated as
Director of Ceremonies.

Author's Note

Reader, I would like to gift you with my sincere gratitude for having purchased or simply taking the time to traverse through my thoughts on public speaking.

I write you this note at a time when challenges of the world seem intent on weighing me down, but I deeply pity any hurdle that comes in the guise of trouble for I have since sought the unseen face of an infinite source of strength.

For the arms of the troublesome world are too under-developed to reach down to the pit of my spirit, I will never be dampened.

I thank the massively faithful Lord God for his countless mercies on me and having facilitated the realisation of this mental portal.

May his plentiful blessings be upon you on your next public speaking endeavour!